A
Broken Heart's
Song

Adam McKim

To those who did me wrong,
truly, I was better off
without you.

Love Never Dies

Lying here on my bed,
Crying tears, for you have fled,
Leaving loose ends never tied —
But for me, love never dies.

You may think that love hurts,
But to me, love is no curse.
Some say they love and they lie,
But for me, love never dies.

You may move on and love again,
But for you, love will not win.
You said feelings change, and I ask why —
Because for me, love never dies.

I'll always wait; you're in my heart.
We're still together, although we're apart.
We can make those loose ends tied,
Because our love should never die.

I Am All Alone

Today is the day,
The best day of my life —
The girl I love the most
Will become my wife.

Everyone has come,
Everyone is there,
To hear us say our vows
About our love and our care.

As the minister reads
From the Holy Book,
I noticed something unusual,
So I turn to take a look.

The church is empty,
Like the inside of a shell.
I turn to my true love —
She is missing as well.

When I wake up,
I'm chilled to the bone.
I cry for my true love,
For I am all alone.

Gates of Love

The gates of love
Require two keys;
Only one is standing there —
That one is me.

Where are you, my love?
Why did you leave?
I know we had problems,
But I still believe.

Others walk by me;
Love they are shown.
There's no possible way
I can walk in alone.

Where is my true love?
Where has she gone?
I am lost and helpless
From dusk till dawn.

The gates of love
Require two keys;
Only one is standing there —
That one is me.

You Are Never There

Every night when I go to bed,
I think of the moments we shared.
Every night I reach for you,
But you are never there.

I dream of you every night.
Where are you, my love, where?
Every night I reach for you,
But you are never there.

I want you in my arms again,
But you are never there.
Can't you see that I still love you
And that I truly care?

I really need your love again;
Let's start over if you dare,
Because every night I reach for you,
But you are never there.

Why

Why did you do this?
Why did you leave,
You ripped my heart out
And left me to bleed.

Why did you leave me?
Why did you go?
I can't live by myself,
I can't live alone.

Why does this happen?
Why is it me?
Don't I deserve love?
Can't I have a need?

Crying and dying
From a broken heart's wound,
Only you can heal me —
I hope you do soon.

Moving On

Moving on is so hard to do;
What can I do? I can't live without you.
Crying in my soul, dying in my heart,
Screaming in my head: why are we apart?

Moving on is tearing me up;
People all around me wishing me luck.
Nobody understands what is going on,
During sleepless nights until the early dawn.

I try to move on, but nothing yet.
Everywhere I turn, I'm caught in a net.
Wandering, staggering, depressed with my life—
Moving on, it cuts like a knife.

Memories

Memories of good times,
Memories of bad times,
Memories of our love —
So many memories.

Memories of us crying,
Memories of us laughing,
Memories of our commitment —
So many memories.

Memories of us hugging,
Memories of us kissing,
Memories of those late nights —
So many memories.

Memories of how we met,
Memories of how you left,
Memories of what you said —
So many memories.

Why did you leave me
with so many memories?
Did you ever realize
that my memories are yours?

Everything we did together
stays within our memories.
I remember getting hurt —
Do you hurt too?

Let's make a new memory
that we can both share —
Let's love again,
with new memories.

Unreal Touch

When I think of you,
I close my eyes and imagine holding you in my arms.
I get so lost in my thoughts that I feel your touch—
That unreal touch.

When I dream of you,
The dream is so real that I never want to wake up.
But I do wake up and realize that touch was, again,
An unreal touch.

How I long to feel your touch,
To hold you in my arms again.
But now every time I feel your touch,
It's always that unreal touch.

So when I go to bed tonight,
I'll dream of you and feel that unreal touch.
When I wake up, I'll think of you and, again,
Feel that unreal touch.

Please Remember Me

As you go on living your life,
Please remember me.
All the times that we shared,
Please remember me.

Don't ever forget our first kiss—
Please remember me.
Don't ever forget the love we had—
Please remember me.

Remember the laughter,
Remember the tears,
Please remember me.
All that I ask from you now
Is to please remember me.

Depressed Heart

Sitting here, drowning in tears,
Wondering why we're apart.
Your love for me has died away
And left me with a depressed heart.

Crying in anger, crying in pain,
Crying in the dark.
Nobody knows what I'm going through
In my depressed heart.

The Show

You give me pain you don't know,
All you see is just a show.
Crying out from deep within,
You see the show about to begin.

Screaming out from my soul,
Your laughter fills this empty hole.
My heart rips out, you still can't see
How much pain you caused me.

Crying, dying on the floor,
Fighting in this heartless war —
A war of anger, war of pain,
Bleed it out, let it drain.

Weakly calling out your name,
My final cry to you in vain.
My breath is shallow, vision blurred,
Silence surrounds me, nothing heard.

Your smile fades and turns to fear,
As this "show" becomes so clear.
Your world has stopped, time is froze,
The curtains of my eyes have closed.

Sorrow fills your time and space,
Tears stream down your lovely face.
My pain was real and now you know —
End of life... end of show.

My Tomb

The four walls around me,
The bed in which I lay.
A lock on my door
Keeps everyone away.

The outside world has nothing,
Not a single thing for me,
For I lost the angel of my life,
An angel as beautiful as she.

I lay within these four walls,
Counting the time go by.
The day comes to an end,
And then I close my eyes.

It is then I dream of her,
As I lie here in my room.
In my dream I leave from here,
This place I call my tomb.

No more walls around me,
No more bed in which I lay.
I have broken from the locks
That kept me here to decay.

In my dream I am with her,
No longer am I sad,
For in my dream she never leaves,
Destroying all we had.

In my dream we are happy,
Our love will only grow,
Reaching to the Heavenly skies,
Leaving the world below.

In my dream I'm full of life,
No longer live in gloom.
My angel pulled me from the trap
Of this place I call my tomb.

I want to stay in this dream,
For when I am asleep.
No longer do I miss her,
No longer do I weep.

I want to stay in this dream,
I never want to wake.
For when I'm here with my angel,
No longer do I ache.

I want to stay in this dream,
Don't ever pull me out.
I want to stay here forever,
For here there is no doubt.

Eventually my eyes will open,
I see the walls of my room.
Once again I'm locked up,
As I lie here in my tomb.

A Broken Heart's Song

A broken heart's song starts out slow,
A confusion of melodies with easy flow.
Keys of a piano play a sad tune,
But nothing compared to what comes soon.

Strings of violins add to the gloom;
The broken heart's song fills the room.
Confusion fades, the hurt settles in—
A Theremin's cry creeps under the skin.

The pain is too much for the broken heart,
As the days go by the anger starts.
The beating of drums while hitting the wall,
The crash of cymbals as you begin to fall.

Confusion to pain, to anger, now hate,
Guitars scream out, the music dilates.
Suddenly it stops, you remember when—
The broken heart's song starts over again.

A Withered Flower

A withered flower you will find,
A symbol of your dying love.
It had lost all its beauty,
That was sent from above.

If you can nurse it back to life,
Unlock its beauty with a key,
Will your love return again,
And find its way back to me?

I Wait in Vain for You

Darkness surrounds my light,
Sadness fills my heart.
The day you came to me,
And ripped us both apart.

You walked away with tears,
You said it wouldn't be long.
You just needed some time
To build yourself up strong.

Friends we had become,
Though I still loved you so.
But never had I dreamed
You would fully let me go.

But that day came,
And now you're with him.
I wanted to end it there,
For he was my best friend.

He came to you while you were weak,
Filled you with his lies.
Made you believe his 'feelings,'
When you are nothing but his prize.

Now he kisses you,
His hands caress your skin.
You hold him in your arms,
Where once I had been.

This I know will not last,
For I told you long ago:
He only lusts after beauty —
This will someday show.

When he's gone, I'll be waiting,
For my love is pure and true.
By then you will be strong again,
I wait in vain for you.

You Should Have Hated Me

The day we met and got together,
The day you changed my life forever.
I was locked up alone; you set me free,
But I say now, you should have hated me.

The day I said that I loved you,
I gave you my heart so pure and true.
You loved me too, that I could see,
But I say now, you should have hated me.

The days we spent with so much fun,
The love we had was second to none.
Why didn't you just let me be?
I wish you would have hated me.

For when you came into my life,
You might as well have raised a knife.
For when that day you walked away,
You plunged it deep, to my dismay.

Now here I sit all alone,
Wishing that I would have known.
I still love you and I will wait,
Even though my heart breaks.

If you would have pushed me away,
And never met me on that day,
I wouldn't have pain to this degree —
If only you would have hated me.

I Hope You Dream of Me

As your day passes by,
Without a single thought of me,
Not a memory of the heart—
You would rather let it be.

Of all the things that come to mind,
I am an absentee.
But when the night falls on you,
I hope you dream of me.

I hope you see me with you,
I hope emotions flow.
I hope you wake up crying,
Because you miss me so.

So as the days go on by,
And it's me you do not see,
When night comes and you sleep,
I hope you dream of me.

Come Back to Me

Come back to me, I beg of you,
Please don't let me go.
This pain is more than I can stand;
It hurts more than you know.

The love I have for you is real,
As real as real can be.
You know this because I still wait,
So long after you left me.

I kiss your picture every night
Before I go to sleep.
As I lie there in my bed,
I then begin to weep.

I cry and cry and cannot stop.
I kiss your picture once again.
I hold it close to my heart,
Where once you had been.

Come back to me, I beg of you,
Please don't go away.
We can make this right again,
Step by step, day by day.

What we had was real,
You say that you agree.
So why throw it all away?
Please, come back to me.

Unsynced Feelings

Love but not loved,
Care but not cared,
Try but not tried,
But still, I share.

Wait but not waited,
Not knowing the fate,
Taken but alone,
Make no mistake.

Pushed but don't push,
Asked but don't ask,
Give but don't take,
This may not last.

Still, I will love,
Still, I will care,
Still, I will try,
I pray you're still there.

A Cursed Gift

I wish I didn't know how to write,
Or how to use a pen.
I wish this skill was forbidden —
The greatest of all sin.

I wish I didn't know how to think,
Or how to use my mind.
If they took it all away,
These words I would not find.

I wish I didn't know how to love,
Or even how to break.
Both of these leave me in fear,
In which I write as I shake.

So take this all away,
Leave me empty in my heart.
I do not want to write again —
It's tearing me apart.

Lies

(The Mirror Sestet)

Lies from you in the sweetest guise,
Guise you were, spilling lies.
Tears on my pillow with all my fears,
Fears of drowning in all my tears.

Pained with truth, my heart is stained,
Stained with lies, my soul is pained.
"I love you," you say — your greatest lie,
Lie about love between you and I.

True, you spoke it, and I said it to you;
You said it as words, I said it as true.
With him you are not — that was a myth,
Myth filled with lies; it's me you're not with.

My Story of Love & Heartbreak
(The Paramirror)

I'll tell you a story about a man,
A man whose life is not so grand.
A story about love and heartbreaks too,
Heartbreaks too painful, sad, and blue.

And blue are the days that will be the worst,
The worst of all time, feelings cursed.
The days will drag on, drained of my glory,
My glory dies in the story.

The story will start out with love, of course,
Of course it's happy, no remorse.
Start out with my heart flying high and free,
And free is my soul...love, the key.

The key which will let all of my guards down,
Guards down... ready for what's around.
Will let the pain in when ready to strike,
To strike at me when it feels like.

Feels like the love is draining from my heart,
My heart was filled 'til she departs.
Love is gone and I feel all of the ache,
The ache of love and then heartbreak.

Lonely

Emptiness in my heart,
Emptiness in my soul,
Emptiness in my life —
Loneliness takes its toll.

Nobody to love me,
Nobody to care,
Trapped in this lonely world,
For nobody is there.

Lonely while standing
In a crowded room,
But screaming to be noticed
When locked in my tomb.

I just want to love
And be loved in return.
Somebody take my heart
And show some concern.

I'm lonely and it hurts,
I'm crying in pain.
Somebody help me —
My heart is slain.

Fill my lonely heart,
Fill my lonely soul,
Fill my lonely life —
Make me feel whole.

I Fell in Love Today

I fell in love today;
It hit me with a sudden shock.
For my heart was sealed tight,
But suddenly there was a knock.

I cracked the door open;
I was too weary to believe.
The emotions all rushed in,
As a love I could perceive.

The feeling was overwhelming;
I could not believe my eyes.
I was filled with happiness
That took over painful cries.

Then suddenly it left;
The door slammed in my face.
My eyes shot wide open,
As my heart began to race.

So love at first sight
Isn't always what it seems.
For I fell in love today,
But was met with shattered dreams.

Love Is a Passionate Pain

Love can be such a wonderful thing,
But beware of the heartaches it can bring.
Love can bring happiness, pure bliss, and joy,
But can also turn your heart into a toy.

Love can be intimate, filling your desire,
But can douse the flame, putting out the fire.
Falling in love can be the ultimate gain,
But if ever it ends, can be a passionate pain.

The War of Love

The end has come, and we have lost—
This battle they call love.
Throughout the wars of our hearts,
A tragic end so undreamed of.

The battle scars are running deep,
The pain I have endured,
For I have left my open heart
Exposed and unsecured.

This war of love—pain and guilt,
Our hearts opened wide.
Only time would know for sure
Whose sword would make the drive.

Now it is I who's on the ground,
Crying out in vain.
A war I hoped to have a draw
Was ended by your aim.

His Love for Her

I sit alone in the dark in fear;
There's a threat upon my life.
His words, so soft and gentle to her,
Are to me as sharp as a knife.

His words of love roll off his tongue,
In waves of forbidden sin.
As her heart flutters like wings of a bird,
His words slice through my skin.

His love pours out from his heart,
As my heart pours out pain.
The more he conveys, the deeper the knife
Plunges through my veins.

His love for her is killing me,
As she is swept away.
Like dawn slicing through night skies,
My heart he will slay.

With the blood spilled from my heart,
As I slowly begin to dispel,
I use the tip from his blade of love,
As I pen my final farewell.

Another Lost Love

I am but a lost and lonely soul,
An empty pit inside searching for love.
A poor man staggering through what they call life—
My life is nothing but heartaches.

My heart has been ripped by the hands of others.
I then find you, a beautiful angel from the heavens.
I feel hope, happiness, wishful thoughts,
But I am not worthy of such love; I am destined to be alone.

Your prince has already arrived on his white horse,
Sweeping you up with his loving words—
Words that have sliced my heart like the blade of a knife.
My heart has yet again been ripped by the hands of another.

The more my heart rips, the more I stagger on,
Limping through this so-called life; love is killing me.
It is time to lock up my heart and say goodbye to love—
It is time to let you go.

I Stand Down

I stand down—
From everything we have been through.
There is no love that can spark for us;
You have already given your love to another.
You have already given away the key to your heart.

I stand down—
From all the dreams, hopes, and wishes I've had.
There is no dream come true, no hope, no granted wishes.
You are already living your dreams and hopes with another;
You already have all of your wishes granted.

For that,
I stand down.

Into the Darkness

I descend back into the darkness
where I seem not to care.
No light of love to cause me pain
and heartaches with tears.
The darkness wipes them all away,
for here my heart is empty.
With this emptiness, there is no emotion,
no feelings…no love.

It is here where I bury myself
deep into the blackened pit,
Alone and not bothered by the
troubles of a love I can't have.
Where the darkness hides
my heart from you, never to be found.
I lock the door to this pit and cast the keys
far away into the night.

As I sit here alone, I think about
the time I have wasted on love,
The years I have lost trying to
make others happy before myself,
The many heartbreaks I have
gone through that tore me apart.
Forget all that pain; though it
may not seem like it, I'm happy now.

This time that I have now is
all mine; forever will it be mine.
The years to come will never be
shared with another again.
No more heartbreaks, for I will
never trust it in the hands of another.
No more pain, only happiness
when I no longer shed tears.

As I sit here alone, the tears
begin to stream down my face.
For all this time I have spent here,
I forgot one thing... memories.
The floodgates open, and they pour
into my dreams, haunting me.
The memories of you surround
me as my cries echo through the pit.

I am now trapped down here
with memories of you; never was I alone.
I have locked myself into my own
tomb of torture for all of eternity.
The sorrows of giving up on what
could have been shatter my heart.
My only hope is that you accept
my love and find the keys to set me free.

Broken

Slipping... from the grips of what's left of hope,
Falling... into a pit of depression and misery,
Hitting... rock bottom as my heart shatters,
Reaching... for that last thread of hope,
Failing... to climb out of my despair,
Defeated... by the reality of truth.
There is no hope left for us.
I have now officially
Been broken
By you.

The Last Thread of Hope

I hang on to the last thread of hope,
For you are slipping away from me.

The thought of losing you pains me
To the very core of my broken heart.

As long as I love you, I'll never let go —
I hang on to the last thread of hope.

Shattered Hopes and Dreams

I'll never forget how we shared with each other
Our future hopes and dreams.

We belonged to each other.

I'll never forget how it was shattered
By him and his dirty schemes.

Death Acceptance

My greatest fear was death—
Until I learned

Love has killed me many times before.

The times have changed;
The tables turned—

I am no longer afraid of death anymore.

Our Love Was Robbed

I sit here broken, confused, shattered beyond repair.
The thought of losing you to him sickens me.
I play our conversations of our dreams through my head—
Rewind...play...pause to cry...play again.

Who is this guy?
What is he trying to do?
When did this happen?
Where did it all go wrong?
Why are we devastated?
How did he come into our lives?

I wonder why he doesn't understand that we were in love.
I can't understand why you still allow him in your life.
I thought he broke your trust with his scheming ways—
Pushes...controls...denies the truth...disrespects.

Who is he to smother you?
What kind of spell did he use?
When did he blind you?
Where did he come from?
Why is he so determined?
How is he ripping us apart?

I know you have a soft and kind heart, it is why I love you.
You live life accepting everyone who enters your circle.
But you need to eliminate the ones with hearts of stone—
Cold...hard...weighs you down...obstruction.

Who does he think he is?
What love comes from stone?
When will you learn?
Where does it start?
Why are you waiting?
How are you going to take control?

I love you deeply from the depths of my heart and soul.
I understand that you are healing from all of this pain.
I just want to be there and give you everything he can't—
Love...happiness...dreams come true...commitment.

Who am I if I did not care for you?
What can I do to help you cast him away?
When do we leave him behind?
Where can we hide from him?
Why don't we do it right now?
How can we take back our love that he robbed us of?

Death from a Broken Heart

A broken heart is more
Than just a feeling.
It takes a toll on the body—
No appetite, chain smoking,
No sleep, awake for days.

When sleep comes, it stays—
22 hours straight.
Wake up, sleep again for 10.
Heart races, panic attacks,
Chest pains, headaches.

I miss you.

Days go by without you,
I don't know what to do.
I'm lost without you.
Where are you? I'm weak.
I need you, I love you.

Help me, my love, save me.
I lay in my bed.
Sleep comes—sleep forever now.
No wake, no pulse,
No pain, peace.

The Other Way Around

If it was the other way around—
If you loved me with all your heart,
If there was another after mine,

If her heart was full of hatred,
If I kept her in my life anyway,
You would leave in a heartbeat.

So why do I stay for you?

Dreams vs Nightmares

Dreams I once hoped
To become a reality
Have lost the fight
To nightmares by fatality.

Shattered by the demons
That haunt my life,
No longer do I dream
Of her as my wife.

I now dream of him
As a devil king,
Claiming my angel,
Clipping her wings.

Dreams that were once
So heavenly bright
Lie broken in hell
Every single night.

The Angel That I'll Never Know

I sit here in pain, for I will never know her —
An angel who I thought was sent to me
From the heavenly skies above,
Whose grace swept my heart right up,

But not in her hands, just flying alone.
I'll never hold her wrapped in my arms.
I'll always have dreams and hopes of her,
But they will always be just that.

I now pen my final farewell to her —
The angel that I'll never know.

She Loves Me in My Dreams

I sometimes wonder
How she really feels inside.
She knows what's in my heart—
My love is implied.

Though she may not love me,
Which is what it seems,
I hope it's enough
If she loves me in my dreams.

I Wait for Her or Death

I vowed to love her 'til the day that I died,
But she may not have the same feelings inside.
I now wait for death in my lonely world,
Heart broken on the floor, twisted and curled.

The days drag on by as I watch her slip away,
No marriage in sight, no children at play.
The nights just as lonely, dreams forever gone,
Waiting for death to take me before dawn.

Though fate is unpredictable, it could change;
Maybe our lives together are future arranged.
But until then, I love her 'til my very last breath —
I'll sit here alone waiting for her or death.

The Pain of Deja Vu

The pain of lost love is all coming back;
It's the same love from years before.
She's swept away again as the pain attacks—
I lose the same girl, the one I adore.

Why must I again go through this?
Twice my love is denied by you.
Just like before, I no longer exist—
I am living the pain of deja vu.

An Undelivered Letter

How are you today?
I hope you are doing well.
It's been awhile, hasn't it,
Since you bid me farewell?

You may not get this;
I don't know if you care,
But I still love you, dear—
I'm still in despair.

While I talk to the wall,
I might as well say—
I still write for you too,
I try to every day.

Along with this message
That you may never see,
I hope that you sometimes,
If even once, think of me.

I think of you every second,
Though you may not know.
You're the highlight of my day,
Though I'm feeling below.

My love, if you get this,
Take a moment to read.
My heart is still yours,
Even though it bleeds.

You may never see this,
But I pray that you do.
I hope that you know—
I'm still waiting for you.

A Distant Goodbye

What was once a distant hope
Has finally met its end.
Many feelings back and forth
In poems we had penned.

The distant hope was twice before,
Over the course of three years.
A fellow poet fought for you
And drowned me in many tears.

Love was painted and purged again
On the canvas of our souls.
The many strokes of every brush
Finally ripped the holes.

In the end, fate disagreed —
Our love we could not rely on.
What was once a distant hope
Is now a distant goodbye.

Western Corruption

I
have had
more lovers than
I would care to admit to
every one of them would have
different ways of breaking my heart
eventually I was driven out of the country
to search for one untouched by western corruption

Though this journey has been full of heartbreak,
I can't close this book without sharing hope.
What follows is the story of finding
"The One."

The One

(The Raven Style)

Long ago, when I was younger, eighteen, single, had a hunger;
For a love that I saw everybody had but never I before.
    As I was searching far and wide, for that someone to be my bride;
    No matter how hard I tried, tried I would for one I adored;
For I would someday find this one, I would find her, this I swore —
      Only this and nothing more.

Ah, before there was a many, the first one, her name was Jenny;
And I had thought that I had finally found the one I asked for.
    My innocence she had taken, and my mind was truly wakened —
    I knew not I was mistaken, mistaken who I adored;
For this one was not my only whom my heart

would love and adore —
     My heart for her did not soar.

There was Tara who came along and our love, it
was very strong;
Thrilled me — filled me with affections thought to
be forevermore;
     For our hearts, they had a tether, we would
always be together —
     Never thought I'd be a nether, that I'd be tossed
out the door —
A few years later, that day came, I was tossed out
of the door —
     My heart again did not soar.

Another Jenny there would be; another love, now
up to three.
I hoped to God this would be the one and only I
adored.
     This girl who was my neighbor, had my heart
beating like a tabour —
     She soon became a labor, labor to keep her was
a chore —
For it was not very long — I was in search for
number four —
     My heart was pained, more and more.

I did not know how to go on, for my heart was nothing but a pawn.

I was stomped and crushed by every single queen I would adore —

All I wanted was to find love, when shall I know of it thereof?

Will I someday swim out of my tears and climb out onto shore?

I want to walk with my love and watch the sunset from the shore —

Merely this and nothing more.

Then one day I met my Sara, my heart was in a new era.

I had finally found the love of my life, to this I swore —

But not a minute would go by that I would catch her in a lie.

I was not the only guy in her life that she would explore —

My heart was only one of the two that my love would explore —

My heart again, on the floor.

Then came along side me Crystal, her love, it shot me like a pistol;

Penetrating my heart all the way down to the very core.
    She was the one I knew for sure, though it would seem from her allure;
    Her siren song was a cure that pulled me through an opened door—
When she found another love, I was tossed again out the door—
    My heart bleeding from the core.

Then here came Chelsea around the bend; introduced by my best friend.
It was a thrilling start of our new love where my heart would soar—
    My friend would then destroy my dream; a shocking side of his scheme;
    To tear away at the seam, the one who I loved and adored—
To take a friendship of seven years and turn it into a war—
    My best friend I now abhor.

I was now twenty-seven years, still drowning deep in all my tears,
From all the past love that I blindly wasted in time before.

Though it may seem I should give in, hang my heart up and raise my chin;

Is it really that much a sin to find the one I adore? —

I must keep fighting for the right for myself to be adored —

Only this and nothing more.

I needed not to be lonely, Becky then became my only.

I travelled far away from my home which I soon did deplore.

She turned out to not be ready, for her heart was so unsteady;

From her own past love already that treated her badly before —

I had to leave my love again, just like many times before —

I wished again — nevermore.

Michelle was the one I confess, was the last here in the U.S.

I was a nothing to her heart but just another boy score.

For two long years I was her lust, then she betrayed all of my trust —

She left me in complete disgust, when I found she was a whore—
She was never ever the one to deserve to be adored—
    For this one, my heart was gored.

I was now thirty and broken, my heart had finally spoken;
Never again would I ever love another, this I swore.
    I would now leave my heart sinking, drain it of all love and shrinking.
    What could I ever have been thinking, searching for one to adore—
I would never again go search for another one to adore—
    My heart would love, nevermore.

I was guarding this heart of mine, when I met this Amy online;
Never met her in person but she was the one, this I swore.
    Though I said I'd love no other, her heart I began to smother—
    But there was also another who fought for her heart to adore—

Neither one of us won the battle, neither one of us adored.

I continued to search more.

This time I was finally done; here, I would never find the one,

It was time for me to go search for one on another shore—

To the Philippines I would go; to Rizza I would come to know;

I had high hopes for us to grow, for this love to be the encore—

Her country she could not forgo, she must stay upon her shore—

I understood, I searched more.

I knew I was getting nearer, my quest could not be more clearer.

I knew my love was somewhere out there on those tropical shores—

For my heart was a complete mess, stained with grief from the U.S.

I had to continue to press—press on to tropical shores—

It would be here that I will find the one who I

would adore—
　　To Philippines—I searched more.

Then Lovely came into my life, my God, I must
make her my wife.
After all I have been through I could never ask for
any more—
　　I had finally found the one; my long search for
true love was done;
　　Two years later we had our son—a family I
adore.
After all of the pain and heartbreaks—a family I
adore.
　　My heart loves—forevermore.

She's always been the perfect wife; never given me
any strife.
I will not have to fight for her heart or tend our
love like a chore.
　　She'll always love me with all she can; for I am
a broken man;
　　She'll always be my biggest fan—never toss me
out the door—
My beautiful wife who came to me from the
tropical shores—
　　She is my forevermore.

There you have it, that's my story—all my pain and all my glory.

I knew that someday I would find my one, this I swore.

The only advice I give you, is for you to keep pushing through.

Do not let those horrible shrews, beat your heart out of the door—

Do whatever it takes to find the one that you will adore—

I suggest—tropical shores.

About the author:

Adam McKim was born and raised in a small town in Missouri, where he still lives today with his wife and son. He began writing in his early twenties and has authored a growing collection of poems and books. When he's not writing, he enjoys quiet moments with family and the continued pursuit of storytelling.